BRITAIN IN OLD P

WEDNESBURY
REVISITED

IAN M. BOTT

SUTTON PUBLISHING LIMITED

Sutton Publishing Limited
Phoenix Mill · Thrupp · Stroud
Gloucestershire · GL5 2BU

First published 1998

Copyright © Ian M. Bott, 1998

British Library Cataloguing in Publication Data
A catalogue record for this book is available from the
British Library.

ISBN 0-7509-2036-X

Typeset in 10/12 Perpetua.
Typesetting and origination by
Sutton Publishing Limited.
Printed in Great Britain by
Ebenezer Baylis, Worcester.

THE BLACK COUNTRY SOCIETY

This voluntary society, affiliated to the Civic Trust, was founded in 1967 as a reaction to the trend of the late 1950s and early 1960s to amalgamate everything into large units and in the Midlands to sweep away the area's industrial heritage in the process.

The general aim of the Society is to create interest in the past, present and future of the Black Country, and early on it campaigned for the establishment of an industrial museum. In 1975 the Black Country Living Museum was started by Dudley Borough Council on 26 acres of totally derelict land adjoining the grounds of Dudley Castle. This has developed into an award-winning museum which attracts over 250,000 visitors annually.

It was announced in August 1998 that having secured a lottery grant of nearly £3 million, the Museum Board will be able to authorize the start of work on a £4.5 million state-of-the-art interpretation centre. This will be known as the 'Rolfe Street Project', named after the street which once housed the Smethwick Baths. The façade of this Victorian building is to be incorporated into the new interpretation centre.

At the Black Country Living Museum there is a boat dock fully equipped to restore narrowboats of wood and iron and different vessels can be seen on the dock throughout the year. From behind the Bottle and Glass Inn visitors can travel on a canal boat into Dudley Canal Tunnel, a memorable journey to see spectacular limestone caverns and the fascinating Castle Mill Basin.

There are 2,500 members of the Black Country Society and all receive the quarterly magazine *The Blackcountryman*, of which 124 issues have been published since its founding in 1967. In the whole collection there are some 1,800 authoritative articles on all aspects of the Black Country by historians, teachers, researchers, students, subject experts and ordinary folk with an extraordinary story to tell. The whole constitutes a unique resource about the area and is a mine of information for students and researchers who frequently refer to it. Many schools and libraries are subscribers. Three thousand copies of the magazine are printed each quarter. It is non-commercial, and contributors do not receive payment for their articles.

PO Box 71 · Kingswinford · West Midlands DY6 9YN

CONTENTS

Grass mowing on Wednesbury golf links, 1935. Greenkeeper Charlie Evans is pictured driving Wednesbury's first motorised tractor, purchased in London from members' subscriptions. The nine-hole course was laid in 1908 on land leased from the Patent Shaft and Axletree Company. Work began in 1951 on the Golflinks housing estate which now covers the area.

Queen Elizabeth II waves to the assembled crowd from the town hall balcony, 24 May 1962. She is joined by the Town Clerk, George Frederick Thompson MA, and the Mayor, Councillor Leonard Waldron. Affixed to the balcony are the municipal coat of arms, granted in 1904. The heraldic lions are taken from the Heronville family coat of arms, twelfth-century Lords of the Manor, while the fesse portrays the symbol of Mars, denoting the iron and steel trades, and two black diamonds, representing the former coal mining industry.

INTRODUCTION

*W*ednesbury Revisited is the latest publication to record something of this ancient industrial town, its people and places. The first book to do so noted the mill, woodland and meadows; but then this was the Domesday Book, written in 1086. The 'Wadnesberie' surveyed then was already a thriving rural community, busily engaged in the daily pursuits of a traditional English manor.

For the next seven hundred years the town saw little change in its green environment, although 'cole pits' were first recorded in 1315 and reference was made to 'Wednesbury Forge' in 1597. During this period the Market Place had developed along with several residential 'town ends' clustered around the main approaches to the town centre. Most of the surrounding land was given over to agriculture, if not woodland. Many of the ancient buildings from this time survived just long enough to be recorded by that wonderful Victorian invention – the camera. Some of these very rare photographs appear in the following pages, alongside other vestiges of old-time Wednesbury captured as late as the 1960s.

The realisation of the area's ample and varied supply of mineral resources, including coal, limestone and iron ore, coupled with the development of mining aids such as the steam pumping engine, meant that by the mid-eighteenth century the pioneers of the Industrial Revolution were beginning to acquire vested interests in the town's pasture and ploughland. Within one hundred years little remained of the once green landscape; instead vast spoil heaps of mining waste obliterated the tilled fields, while acrid smoke and soot belched from forge and furnace, excluding the brightness of daylight and giving rise to the term 'The Black Country'.

Other changes in Wednesbury's topography were brought about by the development of better transport links to surrounding industrial areas and beyond. The first canal to be cut in the district was the Wednesbury Old Canal of 1769. This enabled cargo from the town's coalfields to be transported in great quantities to the industries of Birmingham. Railways arrived in 1837 at Wood Green but soon spread into a network of rival companies and branch lines. Roads also saw major development, such as Thomas Telford's turnpike improvements to the London to Holyhead Road through Wednesbury in 1825.

One of the greatest changes caused by the Industrial Revolution was the dramatic rise in the town's population as thousands of migrants poured in from the surrounding countryside in search of work. Figures more than doubled from 4,160 in 1801 to 8,437 in 1831, and so the multiplication continued. The population explosion brought about the creation of unplanned and haphazard developments of squalid back-to-backs, two-ups-two-downs and courtyard houses. Christened 'slums', these overcrowded and shabby hovels were associated with poverty and disease, with many remaining until the enforcement of slum clearance orders between the wars.

It was owing to the social problems created by the Industrial Revolution that the need arose for a governing body to oversee the basic development of essentials such as water supplies and drainage. These needs were first administered by the Local Board of Health from 1832 until the creation of Wednesbury Corporation. This was effected on 10 July 1886, when the town's first Mayor – Alderman Richard Williams JP – was installed.

One of the first improvements carried out was the creation of a 'green lung' for the benefit of the townspeople. Brunswick Park was opened at Wood Green on 21 June 1887 to celebrate the Golden Jubilee of Queen Victoria. Here 28 acres of pleasure grounds were available for the first time to thousands of residents, most of whom had no private garden.

Many of Wednesbury's public buildings were provided by the generosity of Victorian philanthropists who either resided in or had business connections with the town. One example is the Art Gallery and Museum, in Holyhead Road, which was bequeathed by way of a building fund left by Mary Ann Richards together with the late Edwin Richards Collection of paintings and opened in 1891.

Many of Wednesbury's districts have evolved from ancient times but some came about through the establishment of industry. One such place is Mesty Croft, situated between the town centre and the River Tame. Most of the development here took place in the 1850s when the Wednesbury Building Society established a residential quarter to house the employees of the many tubeworks established here in this period, hence the area's other name, 'New Town'. Most of the original village has now been lost to modern housing developments, only a few industrial buildings and the war memorial being of any age.

Yet more change was to come in the 1960s, most notably with the demise of borough status in 1966. During this decade the remaining old residential areas surrounding the town centre were cleared and outlying modern housing estates were created. Luckily, though, the nucleus of the town survived and many Georgian and Victorian buildings stand today.

The collapse of the steel industry market in the 1980s saw the closure of huge long-established businesses such as Lloyd's Steelworks and the Patent Shaft Company. These sites have now undergone the transition from traditional industrial areas to those of relocated lighter industries and warehousing use mixed with out-of-town retail developments. Most of these have been overseen by the Black Country Development Corporation, which operated with government funds for ten years until 1998 and was also responsible for the creation of the Black Country New Road through the town, and also the £3m restoration of Wednesbury's ancient town centre. The latest development opening later in 1998 is the Midland Metro Light Rail System, operating along the former Great Western Railway route and with headquarters in the town.

And so Wednesbury continues to evolve, the change from old to new always recorded by that ever-present silent witness – the camera!

Patent Shaft Steelworks, seen from the Walsall canal, 1967.

CHAPTER ONE

OLDEN WEDNESBURY

The ancient Wednesbury Manor House is seen in a dilapidated condition in 1897. First mentioned in 1315, it was described in 1884 as a plain, compact and rectangular red brick building in the Tudor style, with a west-facing porch. In the distance can be seen the parish church of St Bartholomew and the Roman Catholic church of St Mary.

Thomas Telford's four-arched Wednesbury Bridge of 1826 is shown in 1897, carrying the London to Holyhead road over the River Tame along Bridge Street. Immediately to the left of the white buildings can be seen Francis Ward's house, from where the preacher John Wesley was taken by the anti-Methodist mob during the Wednesbury riots of 1743. Today a petrol station covers the site.

Opposite Francis Ward's house stood Wednesbury Mill, pictured in 1902. A mill is recorded at Wednesbury in the Domesday Book. Originally a corn mill, its water power was adapted to iron forging in the seventeenth century, but had reverted to its former use by the time of its closure in 1885.

A bustling Wednesbury Market Place is pictured in 1895, one hundred years before the modern trend of out-of-town shopping. The Market Charter was granted by Queen Anne on 9 July 1709 to the Lord of the Manor, John Hoo. An amazing spectacle was witnessed here in 1824, when Moses Maggs, better known as 'Rough Moey', sold his wife Sally and their child for 6s!

Another 1895 view of the market, showing the terracotta façade of the Talbot Hotel, built in 1879, which now houses the post office.

Fraternisation with the Co-operative Retail Society is urged on one of their gala days, held in the Market Place, *c.* 1915. The display exemplifies the virtues of healthy eating.

Meeting Street, named after the Methodist meeting place which formerly stood behind the brick wall to the right, *c.* 1900. The cottage to the left stood on the corner of Lloyd Street, while the building seen at the top of the right-hand side of the road was the Wednesbury Union Workhouse.

Drew's Court, situated off Lower High Street, was one of many poor and overcrowded residential yards swept away by the Slum Clearance Orders of 1935. Today they would attract a new value as 'pretty cottages'.

Wednesbury Wake on land between Ridding Lane and Hydes Road, 1898. Corporation Street now occupies this site. This once boisterous event is still marked by the annual arrival of Pat Collins' travelling fairground in September.

This extremely rare photograph of 1890 shows the Old Library House – to the left of St Bartholomew's church – which for a time housed the Mechanics Institute. Careful examination of the church reveals a breach in its walls (obscured by trees) caused by Basil Champney's relocation of the apse, which wasn't

completed until 1904. The spire of St Mary's Roman Catholic church makes a minute appearance between the chimneys of the Old Library House.

Foundry working conditions have little improved since this 1920 view was taken at Samuel Platt's Kings Hill Foundry, established in 1859. Noticeable is the earth floor, cluttered with tools and castings, and the overhead crane which could travel the length of the foundry. Platt's specialised in the manufacture of pulleys.

Pictured in about 1920 are workers at Edwin Richards Portway Works, New Street, which was established in 1810. Here coach bolts, springs and axles were produced. The Richards family gave the town its art gallery, opened in Holyhead Road in 1891. Some very young faces can be seen in the front row!

Employees of James Russell's Crown Tube Works Bilston Road Depot pose for the camera, *c.* 1910. The Wednesbury tube trade had its origins in the former gun barrel industry and was so widespread that the place was known as Tubetown. Russell's was a vast concern, employing 1,300 hands by 1900.

John Jinks' Forge, 56 Bridge Street, 1897. Here, gas fittings and water cocks were produced. Notice the wooden ventilation traps in the roof.

Victorian hero PC Richard Goldby gained national attention in 1897 – when twenty-four years old – through his recovery of the body of night watchman Thomas Hodgkiss, aged seventy-one, who perished after falling into a burning chasm in Old Park Road, Kings Hill (caused by spontaneous combustion of the underlying coal seam) and being roasted to death. This hideous accident occurred on the evening of 14 April. PC Goldby's bravery was rewarded with the presentation of a medal by the Prince of Wales.

The scene in Old Park Road, the morning after the unfortunate night watchman's death. The harness and ladder by which PC Goldby descended into the fiery pit can be seen as smoke issues from a burning fissure behind. Known locally as 'wildfire', the effects of this spontaneous combustion have been witnessed by the author on wasteland, as late as 1976.

Wednesbury Grand Division of the Order of the Sons of Temperance line up for this photograph of 1907. These abstainers from alcoholic beverages had a meeting hall in Stafford Street. The man on the far right (marked X) is A. Jenkins.

Eliza Platt stands on the right, with a friend in the grounds of the family home, The Shrubbery, in Wood Green Road, *c*. 1900. The pony would have regularly transported family members across the town by trap.

The Three Tuns, Union Street, was kept by Herbert Riley when pictured, 1904. Shutters were a feature of most town centre buildings at this time, and had a certain appeal that their modern roller counterparts lack.

This rare picture shows the Queen's Head, which was situated in Queen Street on the corner of Queen's Place. William King Townend is listed as licensee in a directory of 1905. His name appears on the board above the entrance. The plaque to the left reads 'R.W. Queen Place, A.D. 1838'.

CHAPTER TWO

THOSE WERE THE DAYS

All smiles on an evening out for Prodorite employees and their partners, 1958. Foreground, left to right:
Jean Riley, Pamela Beech, Mary Haden, -?-, Enid Bishton, Jean Maczka, -?-, Marian Maczka.

Wednesbury Conservative and Unionist Association Grand Fête and Gala was held at Lea Brook Grounds on 22 August 1925. Timber merchant C. Walsh Graham's wagon is seen gaily disguised as a 'Night Club Revellers' float. The balloons advise us to shop at Lewis's for toys. Sisters Elsie and Dora Collett are pictured with collecting tins, third and fourth from left.

Residents of Handley Street celebrate VE Day, 1945, with a street party. Lilian Higgs (centre) serenades the group with her banjo. The little girl dressed in a nurse uniform is Brenda Janes. Betty Janes stands second from the right.

Civilian workers enjoy a ladies' wheelbarrow race in the yard of the fire station, Ladbury's Lane, *c.* 1940.

Family and friends join Margaret Hollingsworth at her twenty-first birthday party, 20 July 1947. Miss Hollingsworth is seated (centre) with a buttonhole of flowers. Hollingsworth's were a well-known firm of butchers.

The Coronation of Queen Elizabeth II was celebrated in Johnson Road, Friar Park, with a dance in the street, 2 June 1953.

Meanwhile, the pupils of Holyhead Road Infants School entertained their parents with a display of maypole dancing.

Children raise a laugh at the Lime Road street party, 2 June 1953. The variety of dining chairs makes an interesting picture.

A delicious spread awaits the residents of Coleman Road, 2 June 1953. In the background can be seen the Albert Pritchard Nursery School.

Party hats advertising Brooke Bond Tea are
worn by children at the Beech Road street
party, 2 June 1953.

The television is unplugged for a while so that children can enjoy their Christmas party at the Civil
Defence Club, Hawthorn Road, c. 1960.

Brother and sister Barry and Pat Beesley ride a two-seater tricycle along the passageway connecting George Street to Dudley Street, 1941.

Teachers and pupils build a giant snowman in the yard of St James' School during the severe winter of 1947. Playtime had come early after the heating boilers had broken down.

Members of Wednesbury Civil Defence quench their thirst on a hot summer's day in 1955. Back row, left to right: Albert Russell, -?-, George Jellyman, Jack Bourne, Bill Bourne. Front row: Norman Russell, Billy Collett, Tom Russell, Joe Simpkin, Gordon Davies.

Busy bar and waiting staff pause for the camera at the Ski Rooms in the Anchor Hotel, Holyhead Road, 1956. Maisie Lee is seen, far right, behind the till.

Licensee's wife 'Ria' Noakes keeps an eye on proceedings from the serving hatch at the Britannia Inn, Holyhead Road, in 1950.

Five imbibers enjoy an evening out on the town, *c.* 1960. Left to right: Harry Wedgbury, Jack Mullender, -?-, Sidney Mullender, -?-.

Colleagues gather for the Prodorite Annual Dinner, 1956. To the left waitresses prepare to serve the soup

starters. Prodorite, based in Leabrook Road, made specialist floor and wall coverings.

A basket of pigeons is one of the props used for the Civil Defence Club Christmas fancy dress parade, Hawthorn Road, *c*. 1960. Maria Mullender is seated in the centre, with a baby's feeding bottle full of rum.

Queen Elizabeth II's Silver Jubilee of 27 July 1977 was marked by the residents of Foley Street with a street party. The chairs appear to have been borrowed from a local school.

CHAPTER THREE

AROUND THE
TOWN CENTRE

Open air stalls in the Market Place, 1950. The market was removed to a purpose-built covered site in the nearby Shambles in 1970. The canvas canopies are stamped 'Borough of Wednesbury Markets'.

The George V Coronation clock tower is prominent in this view of the Market Place, 1912. The four illuminated faces were made by the Synchronome Clock Company of London and placed in the brick and York stone tower, designed by C.W.D. Joynson and built by Summerhill and Jellyman. The dedication service took place on 9 November 1911. It is regulated by a master clock in the town hall and originally chimed the hour.

The original Old Golden Cross Inn, to the right of the clock tower, 1912. The wing housed under the 'cat-slide' roof was occupied by dental surgeon J.B. Blain, whose hours are stated as 9 a.m. to 8 p.m daily. The Old Golden Cross has recently been renamed the Pig and Trumpet.

Here, the Market Place is viewed from the Five Ways junction, 1950. The piece of street furniture seen left, outside Wooltons, was a police emergency telephone. When the light flashed blue, the local 'bobby' would use his key to answer the call. The parked van belonged to the Wednesbury Laundry Company.

More market stalls feature in this picture, 13 February 1965. A delivery van is parked outside Stanton's Bakery, to the right. The break in the buildings was caused by the demolition of the George and Dragon Hotel the previous month.

Union Street, 13 March 1965. The shops in view occupied the frontage between Little Camp Street and Camphill Lane, now the site of the Union Shopping Centre.

Fishmonger Sidney Powell awaits customers at his open-fronted marble slab, trading as Stanton's, in this picture of Union Street, 1967. Wassall's shoe shop is hung with their products to the left.

This picture, taken a little further along in 1969, shows more of the Union Street names – such as Lowe's Cornshop, Austin Sports, Wolverson's Butchers, Desbes Drapers and O'Connell's Fruiterers.

Another Union Street view, this time in 1974 and showing Decorate Paints. The street was pedestrianised in 1993.

Russell Street, 26 January 1965. Clearance of its old buildings had already begun. A *News of the World* poster above H.L. Roberts' newsagent's reads 'Story of the horse dopers – amazing confessions!' The steeple visible to the right belonged to St John's church, Lower High Street.

When newsagents H.L. Roberts' turn for demolition came, they moved to a 'temporary' building across the road. This, pictured on 1 February 1967, is now home to the RSPCA clinic. The original St John's School can be seen to the left. The tower crane faintly seen in the background was engaged in the construction of Russell House flats.

Young Clara Bott proudly shows her doll's pram while Elizabeth Ann Bott (Annie) keeps a careful watch through the window of the family general store in Camp Street, 1927. The diamond pattern blue brick pavers were once commonplace but are now very rare.

Spring Head, looking down into the Market Place, 1 February 1967. Beyond the *Express and Star* newspaper office can be seen the Wadsworth Café, once popular dining rooms.

Upper High Street, showing the demolition of the Grapes public house, March 1967. This site remains undeveloped to this day.

Most of these Upper High Street shops, pictured in 1966, were swept away for construction of the Northern Orbital by-pass in 1969. The clock on Joseph Leslie Beardmore's watch repair shop remains today. All the buildings left of this have disappeared.

These High Bullen buildings, pictured in 1968, are visible in the distance on the photograph above. From the left can be seen George Croft Steelworks, the Wednesbury Garage, Savoy Artistic Furnishers and the Rising Sun, Trouse Lane.

The Rising Sun, 1 Trouse Lane, alongside the Blackpool 'chippie', 1967. Although the chip shop has long gone, the Rising Sun survives as an elderly persons' rest home.

Joseph Leslie Beardmore's watch repair shop, 6 Trouse Lane, before the business moved to Upper High Street. Mr Beardmore had the added tasks of maintaining the clocks in Brunswick Park and the Market Place, as well as winding St Bartholomew's church clock daily.

Johnny Farmer's drapery store, Trouse Lane, *c.* 1960. The date of establishment (1855) is clear on the wall. The Atkinsons ale sign visible to the right belonged to the Fortune of War, which stood on the corner of Wellcroft Street. This pub name was an allusion to the once extensive trade in the town of gunmaking.

Harold Stackhouse's newsagents, 40a Trouse Lane, December 1925. A poster for fireworks still hangs above the doorway as a newsboy and newsgirl set off on their rounds. The male chauvinist *Reynolds News* poster declares that 'women are bad motorists'!

A worker from the Gaumont Picture House, Walsall Street, clears snow from the front of the premises, *c.* 1950. In the background can be seen the old Wednesbury swimming baths of 1878 and the Education Offices of 1913. New swimming baths opened in High Bullen in 1974.

Oakeswell End, seen here in 1959, is actually a part of Walsall Street, so called because of the former presence of the ancient Oakeswell Hall. To the left of the telephone box can be seen Jackson's Chemist and the original Oakeswell post office. The former has been demolished, while the latter survives as a day nursery.

CHAPTER FOUR

CAUGHT IN THE ACT

An amateur dramatic production is staged at the Baptist church, Holyhead Road, in 1952. The players, left to right are: -?-, Sidney Hill, -?-, Alan Hill, Elizabeth Wainwright, Annie Hinkinson, -?-, Janice Wainwright, Malcolm Tromans and Ivy Wainwright.

Born on 25 February 1912 at 11 Hollies Drive, actor Richard Wattis became a household name through many film roles (once with Marilyn Monroe) and a regular appearance as cranky neighbour Mr Brown in *Sykes*, the television comedy, with Hattie Jacques and Eric Sykes. The son of Wednesbury Corporation's Rating and Valuations Officer, Cameron Tom Wattis, he was first educated at the King Edward School, Birmingham, followed by Bromsgrove School. Another of his fondly remembered roles was as the 'Man from the Ministry' in the St Trinian's films. Sadly he died in London in 1975.

The Hippodrome Theatre, Upper High Street, was first opened in 1891 as the New Theatre Royal, seating 1,500 and designed by the Wednesbury architect C.W.D. Joynson. During the Second World War it had a spell as a British Restaurant.

Local businessman and theatre lover Hubert John Barlow, pictured in 1953, owned the Hippodrome in post-war years and traded as Magnet Entertainments. His other main concern in the town was the Mounts Steelworks, which also operated a brick-making plant. Keen on all local issues, he was Mayor of Wednesbury in 1931 and also served as a county councillor.

This superb picture shows the Wednesbury Repertory Company performing *The Pied Piper of Hamelin* on the Hippodrome stage, 1950s. Many of these young thespians found lodgings with local theatre-going families.

Wednesbury Hippodrome manager Mr W.A. Butler stands behind six seated players from the Wednesbury Repertory Company as they join spectators at the cricket ground within Wednesbury Sports Union at Wood Green, 1953. Far left, seated below the scoreboard, are Mr Robert Davidson, headmaster of St Bartholomew's School and Margaret Hayward. The line up continues: -?-, Pauline Brandt, Martin Landau, -?-, John Jarvis, Robert Hartley.

To the rear can be seen the original wooden sports pavilion dating from 1913 and replaced with purpose-built premises in 1964. Wednesbury Sports Union was founded in 1936 to encourage the development of amateur sport in the town.

In 1957 a theatre club was formed to help promote the Hippodrome and carry out tasks such as scenery painting and light maintenance. When it was decided by the management to close the theatre, early in 1959, theatre club members launched 'Operation Lifeboat' in an attempt to revive interest. Here, campaigners are seen distributing leaflets outside the theatre. Ray Wood is standing to the right.

Sadly the Hippodrome was deemed no longer viable and closed in April 1959. Planning permission for conversion to a car sales showroom was granted in September 1959; however, the building was pulled down in the 1960s to make way for a supermarket development.

Actress Jill Simcox was born on 1 October 1935, the daughter of Wednesbury dentist Jack Simcox. Her childhood home was in Brunswick Park Road before the family moved to The Squires, 5 Walsall Street. Educated at Ethel Davey's Woodland Grange School in Wood Green Road, then Adcote, Shropshire, she later studied at the Royal Academy of Dramatic Art. Now living in Middlesex, she is remembered for her TV roles as Sister Arnold in *Emergency Ward Ten* and farmer Linda Ash in *Crossroads*. Another famous ex-pupil of Woodland Grange is the actress Sue Nicholls, who plays Audrey Roberts in *Coronation Street*.

Pupils from Wodensborough High School, Hydes Road, tread the boards for the 1979 production *It'll Be Alright On the Night Snow White*. Left to right: Ian Banner, Leigh Rowbottom, Peter Tapper-Gray and 'Master of Disguise' Stewart Gill.

The chorus line from the above production dance through their 'sailor routine'. On the players' caps is written 'HMS *Wodensborough*'.

Holyhead Road Baptist church is the setting for this 1952 nativity play. The winged Angel Gabriel (centre) is Pat Beesley.

Pupils of St James' School stage a re-enactment of the Crucifixion at St James' church, *c.* 1950. The school and church are both to be found in the aptly named St James Street.

CHAPTER FIVE

DOWN YOUR WAY

Foley Street, 1967, showing the houses on the right that were demolished in the 1980s. Centre of the picture is the Crown Stores, Brunswick Park Road, originally a public house named the Isle of Man Inn, but today known as the Oakeswell off-licence.

Church Steps snaked its way from Trouse Lane, up the hill to the top of Church Street. The passageway is seen here on the wintry morning of 14 February 1966.

The stone steps that christened the passage were located further up the hill and are seen here in 1900. Similar steps and railings survive in nearby Squires Walk.

The entrance to Church Steps can be seen here in March 1966, between Noon's grocery store and O'Connell's greengrocers, Trouse Lane. The corner of the Rising Sun public house can be seen in the left foreground.

Ladbury's Lane, pictured here in about 1960, ran from High Bullen to Church Street. St Bartholomew's Church School can be seen at top left. The whole street was swept away in 1965 to create the open space known as Church Hill Gardens.

This very rare view of 1930 shows the old houses in Ethelfleda Terrace, which were replaced by the Ethelfleda Memorial Gardens in 1953. Princess Ethelfleda, daughter of King Alfred the Great, was said to have fortified the site in the year 916.

A third thoroughfare climbing the hill was Earp's Lane, linking Upper High Street to Church Street at the Woden Inn. Empty homes await the bulldozer in this early 1960s view. To the right can be seen the Rialto Cinema, advertising the film *I'm All Right, Jack*.

Woden Passage, 13 March 1968. It linked Holyhead Road to Stafford Street with Albert Street passing between. The section between Holyhead Road and Albert Street now forms part of the police station car park. A fine pair of Victorian gas lamps stand in the passage.

Bridge Street is seen here in 1967, showing the eighteenth-century coaching inn, the Red Lion, which was demolished in March 1983. Only the limestone-clad Lloyds Bank remains today, St John's church behind having been demolished in 1985.

Holyhead Road at its junction with Kings Cross, September 1960. The Kings Court and Queens Gardens development replaced these old buildings in 1964.

Loxdale Street has few houses remaining in this 1965 view, which also shows the site of George Street. The town's bus station now occupies this site.

Holyhead House, 172 Holyhead Road, 26 January 1965. This was the house of Mayor (1906–8) Alderman John Handley and his sister, Jane, who gave the two granite horse troughs which now stand either end of Union Street. It was also the childhood home of the author's father.

These houses stood along the Holyhead Road between Loxdale Street and Russell Street. Also on this picture of 5 February 1965 can be seen 1 Loxdale Street (left), the former home of poor law medical officer Dr Edward Alfred Dingley JP (1860–1948).

Wednesbury Corporation refuse carrier no. 6 makes its way down Meeting Street, March 1966. The houses with attics beyond Mark Road were known as Husbands Buildings.

Great Western Street is one of the widest roads in the town, a necessity because of the high volume of goods vehicles that needed access to the railway. Just discernible on this picture of 3 May 1970 is the faded advertisement for the long de-licensed Brunswick Inn, named after the Patent Shaft and Axletree Company's Brunswick Ironworks, seen in the distance.

The boundary of Wednesbury with Tipton at Leabrook, March 1966. In the distance, the Great Western Railway line crosses Leabrook Road alongside the Patent Shaft Steelworks. The Boat Inn was so named because of its close proximity to the Walsall and Monway Branch canals. The 'ashes for sale' sign refers to cinders (burnt coal), which were very useful for repairing driveways.

George Cecil Mallam is pictured on 28 April 1970 at his traditional corner shop, which had the Wednesbury postal address of 65 Leabrook Road, despite being a few hundred yards over the borough boundary. The premises were demolished in November 1977.

Piercy Street, Mesty Croft, at its junction with Hydes Road, 2 March 1967. W.S. George sold petrol here from pavement-mounted pumps.

This view from Piercy Street is obtained from across the London and North Western Railway cutting at Hydes Road, 2 March 1967. The whitewashed building in the centre was the Rising Sun public house.

Oxford Street, Mesty Croft, from the Hydes Road end, 2 March 1967. The whitewashed shop displaying the Walls ice cream sign was no. 7, Ward's general stores.

Further along Oxford Street in the direction of Friar Park, 2 March 1967. The parked cars are outside the Foresters Arms public house, which is where the Mesty Croft school caretaker's house now stands.

Hollies Drive, pictured here in 1912, was originally the toilsome pathway to The Hollies mansion house, seen crowning the road. The public library, on the left, was opened in 1908, a gift of philanthropist Andrew Carnegie on land provided by Alderman John Handley JP.

Walsall Street at its junction with Hydes Road, 1971. In the centre can be seen the original Oakeswell surgery, served by Doctors Frost, Duesbury, Blackwell and Huey at this time.

An almost deserted Wood Green Road, looking in the direction of Wednesbury town centre, 5 February 1967. The buildings on the left are Dolobran and The Limes, two former family homes turned into the County Commercial College. This section of road is now a stretch of busy dual carriageway leading to junction 9 of the M6 motorway.

Ridding Lane, showing the Dog and Partridge public house at the junction with Addison Street, 2 March 1967. The building to the left of the row housed Nutt's grocery store.

Victoria Street, seen here on 13 March 1968, linked the Holyhead Road to the Great Western station, seen in the distance alongside the Great Western Hotel. The Prince Regent public house stood on the corner of Albert Street. Opposite can be seen Hickinbottom's 'Electric' Bakery. One of their delivery vans is just emerging from Stafford Street. On the horizon can be seen one of the cooling towers at Ocker Hill Power Station.

A view of Albert Street looking towards Dudley Street, 13 March 1968. Before the creation of large housing estates most of Wednesbury's population lived in such streets, close to the town centre.

CHAPTER SIX

FACES IN THE CROWD

The Mayor, Alderman Leonard Whitehouse JP, tosses a pancake into the crowd at the Market Place, Shrove Tuesday 1952. Seen on the right, attending the Mayor, is Bruce Bennett. Beyond can be seen the Green Dragon Hotel, which was de-licensed in 1960. The tiny brick structure to the left of the phone booths was a police box.

Sunday School Anniversary is celebrated at the United Methodist Free Church in Ridding Lane, 1950s. Someone has worked very hard at polishing the balcony!

Appointing a 'Boy Bishop' was a ceremony practised at St Luke's church, Alma Street, Mesty Croft, seen here in 1949. For this revived medieval custom the 'Bishop' was elected from the choir by secret ballot and installed in a ceremony on the Sunday nearest the feast of St Nicholas – the patron saint of choirboys.

St Bartholomew's School, Church Street, is the setting for this 1950s nativity play. Kitchen foil and tea towels have been used to make angels' and shepherds' costumes.

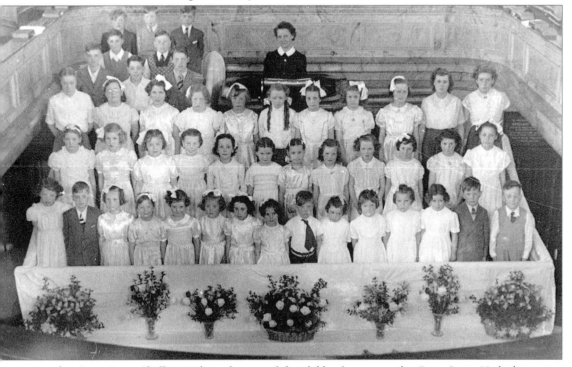

Preacher Sister Doris Chaffer stands to the rear of this children's group at the Camp Street Methodist Sunday School Anniversary, 1952.

Sunday School Anniversary is again celebrated, this time during the 1920s at Leabrook chapel. Here the original church can be seen, surrounded by the chimney stacks of the nearby Patent Shaft works.

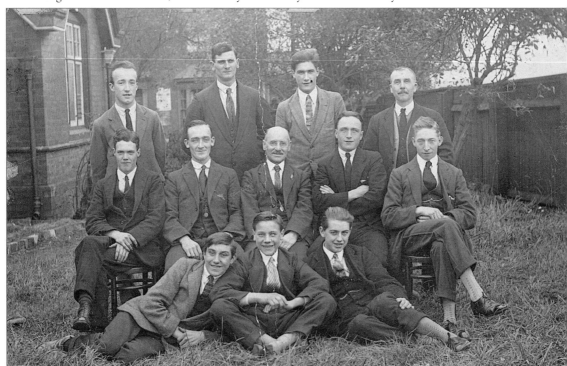

In the grounds of the 'new' Leabrook chapel, *c.* 1935. Back row, left to right: Vic Pittaway, Harold Neale, -?-, Ben Thorpe. Middle row: Ernie Hayfield, Bill Lowe, ? Pickering, Wilf Smith, Sam Higgins. Front row: Jack Garner, Harold James and Frank Pickering.

The Masonic Hall in Russell Street is the backdrop for this picture of the members of Wednesbury St John's Ambulance Brigade, 1931.

Wednesbury Home Guard, probably at the 'Sports Union' ground, Wood Green, *c.* 1944. Many of the larger factories also had their own contingent.

Associate concerns of the Patent Shaft & Axletree Company's Brunswick Ironworks were the Monway and Old Park plants. These themselves were subdivided into various specialised departments. Here, pictured in 1919, are the workforce of the Monway Engineering Depot. The sooty faces of some suggest they worked in close proximity to boiler flues.

Workers from the Old Park plant line up for a picture, 1921. Here, in 1885, was made the world's first all-steel bridge, which was sited at Benares, over the River Ganges. Its total span was 3,518 ft and it weighed in at 6,500 tons. John William Welch stands third from left, back row, while Albert Leslie Allen is seated fourth from left, middle row.

Wednesbury Forge at Wood Green is first mentioned in a document dated 1597. Edward Elwell established his edge tool manufactury here in 1817, where the world-famous Spear and Jackson gardening tools are still made today. Employees are pictured here in about 1938, during the demolition of one of Elwell's original forge buildings.

Staff from Isaiah Oldbury Ltd at the Reliance Works, Oxford Street, Mesty Croft, c. 1938. Some of the women are wearing lopsided berets, fashionable at this time. Founded in 1861, the firm made coach fittings before later turning to the production of trailers.

Wednesbury actress Jill Simcox makes a dash for her marriage to Twickenham actor Malcolm Gerard, at St Bartholomew's church, 20 June 1965. Her arrival had been delayed by ten minutes when the crowd of over 2,000 spectators caused the approach to be blocked. Her father, Wednesbury dentist Jack Simcox, follows directly behind, the close proximity of his top hat making an amusing picture.

Mayoress Mrs Collins turns the key in the door to declare the Sons of Rest building open, 3 November 1938. The Foley Street building has been providing a place of recreation for the retired menfolk of Wednesbury for sixty years now.

The founding membership line up for the camera on the newly laid turf of the Sons of Rest, 3 November 1938. The building is ideally sited, being in one corner of Brunswick Park.

Officers and committee of the Wednesbury Bridge Social Club, Bridge Street, 1953. Back row, left to right: A. Maddox, J. Earp, J. Rogers, J. Nightingale, W. Cousins, S. Malpass, T. Wood, J. Gutteridge. Front row: T. Brookes, S. Brookes, S. Silk, F. Wright, T. Edkins, W. Bourne, J. Moran, T. Whitehouse.

Civil Defence members gather in the town hall for an evening of dance, c. 1948.

Mesty Croft Darby and Joan Memorial Hall committee members on 19 September 1957. Standing, left to right: Mrs Ingram, Councillor Mark Allen, Mrs Foster, Basil Smerdon, Mrs Day, Mayor Councillor Walter Morgan, Mayoress Mrs Morgan, William Cox, Miss Walford, Mr Ashford, Mrs Reeves. Seated, left to right: Mr Bowers, Sam Stevenson, Revd Walter Sidwell, Alderman George Price, Alderman Ethel Price.

Pupils and their form teacher, Mr Timmins, pictured in 1950 at Joseph Edward Cox Junior School, Dorsett Road, Friar Park, which has recently been renamed Priory School. Prior to boundary changes of 1931, most of the Friar Park district belonged to West Bromwich.

Teacher Mrs Millard joins infants at St Bartholomew's School for a class photograph, 1957. The playground wall is made up of foundry waste, known as slag.

Engineering cadets take a break from studies in 1943, near the County Technical College, Walsall Street, originally known as the County Metallurgical and Engineering Institute.

Mesty Croft men group around a returned First World War hero, seen in the centre of the second row, 1919. The field they are pictured in was to the rear of the Imperial Tube Works, Friar Street. Access was gained over the River Tame (or 'Brown Brook') by way of a brick footbridge at the bottom of Elwell Street.

Members of the Ladies Auxiliary of the Wednesbury and Darlaston Licensed Victuallers Association, at the Park Royal Brewery, 24 May 1956. In the second row fifth and sixth from the left are Maisie Lee and Kate Garbett.

Mesty Croft residents watch the parade go by on carnival day, August 1956. Behind can be seen A. Smith's general stores, which stood at the corner of Alma Street and Piercy Street.

Twelve months later it's carnival day again. This time party goers are joined by the Mayor and Mayoress, Councillor and Mrs Walter Morgan, seen here at the Vine Inn, Alma Street, August 1957. One resident displays the donations from the street collection.

Councillors and carnival committee members gather on the steps of the Coronation clock, Market Place, to present the ox picked for roasting on carnival day, 24 September 1931. The unfortunate beast was cooked at 3 p.m. that afternoon. Standing in a central position below the clock plaque is the Mayor, Councillor Hubert John Barlow.

Wednesbury scouts are joined at the Central railway station by the Mayor, Councillor L.B. Gardner and the Revd Alexander Bunn Lavelle of St Bartholomew's church, 1949, before setting off on a holiday to Switzerland.

CHAPTER SEVEN

A STROLL IN THE PARK

Brunswick Park was opened by the Mayor Alderman Richard Williams JP on 21 June 1887, to mark the Golden Jubilee of Queen Victoria. Designed by William Barron and Son of Borrowash, Derbyshire, its 28 acres were created from pit mounds purchased from the Patent Shaft and Axletree Company, and named after their Brunswick Ironworks.

The Park Lodge provides a backdrop to this delightful picture of a school outing to the park, *c.* 1908. The lodge was the residence of the park keeper, Mr Joseph Pym.

Park Keeper Joseph Pym, seen here in 1902, joined by young friends around the Children's Drinking Fountain, a gift from Charles Southern JP in 1889. Water issued from an upturned jug held by an infant bronze. When removed for the war effort in 1939, it was replaced by a limestone successor.

A good show of patriotism is the order for the day, as the Coronation of King George V is celebrated on 22 June 1911. The framework in the distance was probably for fireworks.

The lake, pictured in 1912, was known as Barron's Pool after its designer. It formed a crescent shape complete with two ornamental islands. Problems with leakage caused it to be drained between the wars, and it was replaced with a paddling pool and children's play area.

Just discernible in this 1925 photograph are the pair of seating shelters, positioned on The Mount, to give extensive views over the park. To the right can be seen the pillar clock, donated by William Hunt in 1911 to celebrate the Coronation of George V. The pillar was cast by Hardy Padmore and Company of Worcester and the clock supplied by the Synchronome Company of London.

The original bandstand from 1887 was, like the shelters, of a rustic construction that weathered badly. Soon after this picture was taken in 1925, the structure had to be replaced. The location of this earlier bandstand was near to the pillar clock, as can be seen in the top picture.

Members of Wednesbury Choral Society gather at the 'new' bandstand in 1959, in preparation for an open air concert. The bandstand was presented by Arthur H. Johnson OBE, from Northampton, on a specially prepared central site in 1928. Here a terraced amphitheatre was created to accommodate seated audiences, each level being shored up with furnace slag, the residue of smelted ironstone. In 1929 Mr Johnson made the additional gift of two bronze lamps in the form of nude female figurines, gracing the steps to the octagonal edifice atop the brick plinths.

A programme of concerts was arranged annually by the Parks and Cemeteries Committee giving free use of the enclosure. The bandstand is the only surviving example of its kind in the modern borough of Sandwell. In 1994, due mainly to the efforts of Ms Sue Whitehouse, the park and bandstand were added to the English Heritage Parks and Gardens Register as being of national importance.

Fifth from left stands choirmaster Frank Lloyd while Arthur Spittle is seen against the balustrade, eighth from the left.

The northern approach to the bandstand, 1950. Pathways were lined with a double row of cobblestones and flower beds were protected by border fencing. The Council minutes record the prosecution of two young girls in May 1960 for picking tulips!

The whalebone arch, seen here in 1950, graced the approach to the pavilion. When one bone developed a fracture at its base in 1963, the pair had to be removed for public safety.

Opened in 1926, the pavilion is viewed here from across the putting green in the 1930s. In later years a 'crazy golf' course was laid on the green.

The pavilion was a very popular attraction within the park, serving light refreshments and housing public conveniences. This photograph dates from about 1938. Severe structural damage caused by mining subsidence necessitated its demolition in 1990.

Mesty Croft residents Mr and Mrs Samuel Bellingham, celebrating the Silver Jubilee of King George V and Queen Mary, 5 May 1935. An entrance opposite the end of Crankhall Lane gave people of this district convenient access to the park.

The newly created children's paddling pool, photographed in 1931, was built on the site of the park lake. This in turn is now occupied by the children's play area, a new pool having been constructed nearby. Through the trees can be seen the chimney stack belonging to the South Staffordshire Waterworks pumping station, Brunswick Park Road.

Members of Wednesbury Civil Defence present a demonstration of field cookery during the Horticultural Show, 1955.

Jack Mullender plays his 'wood' watched by three competitors on the bowling green, c. 1955. Behind can be seen one of the glasshouses in the maintenance yard.

Friends Ann Hollingsworth and Judith Farmer enjoy the Horticultural Show in the park, 1957.

Riders prepare for the gymkhana in the main arena at the Horticultural Show, 1960. Housed inside the marquee are household appliances for the 'electricity show'.

CHAPTER EIGHT

WEDNESBURY
BOROUGH NEWS

John Stonehouse MP celebrates his Wednesbury election win at the town hall, April 1956. Left to right: Sam Stevenson, Mary Stevenson, John Stonehouse MP, Merl Burrows, Tom Burrows and Les Stevenson.

A patriotic welcome is given to HRH Edward Prince of Wales on 13 June 1923, as the Royal motorcade travels along Wood Green Road in the direction of the town centre.

HRH Prince George KG is attended by members of the town council, 24 April 1933. Here, in the council chamber of the town hall, he was entertained to a civic luncheon.

Janice Nicholls sits alongside fiancé Brian Meacham, as another broadcast is made of pop review show *Thank Your Lucky Stars*, from the Alpha Television Studios, Birmingham, 1963. The couple, in the centre, had just announced their engagement. Janice first achieved fame after joining the show in 1962 and declaring in her strong Wednesbury accent 'Oi'll give it foive'. This became a national catchphrase as she made hundreds of television appearances with stars such as The Beatles, Cliff Richard, Cilla Black and Lulu.

She was born at 27 Moor Street, Mesty Croft, on 24 January 1946, before the family moved to the nearby Friar Park district. Schools attended were Tameside Infants and Juniors followed by Heronville Girls (now Holyhead Road Juniors). Once, her father caused great consternation by stirring paint with a drumstick given by Ringo Starr! The couple married at St Paul's church, Wood Green, Wednesbury, on 11 September 1965. Today they have two grown-up children, and still reside in Staffordshire.

Station officer T. Phillips (left) shakes the hand of Officer Ainsworth as he presents him with a cutlery set and clock at Wednesbury old fire station, Ladbury's Lane. This picture dates from the Second World War, evident by the taped glass of the maintenance garage windows.

Firewomen Margaret Danks and Lottie Wallis outside the fire station garage, c. 1942. During the Second World War women had to take on the then traditional male role of fire-fighting. Note the pile of sandbags reflected in the garage door glass.

Fire-fighters tackle the fierce Quilliam Bag Works blaze, which was one of a series of severe fires during the 1960s. The Great Western Hotel can be seen in the left background.

Firemen damp down the smouldering remains of the Potters Lane factory, where the manufacture of jute sacks was a speciality.

Wednesbury Home Guard officers and corporals guard the entrance to the town hall, Holyhead Road, which was used as an Emergency Information Bureau during the Second World War. Standing left foreground is Tom Hollingsworth, a Wednesbury butcher.

Civil Defence members lead the Remembrance Sunday parade through the Market Place, *c.* 1955. Shops nos 1 to 5, behind, were demolished in February 1989.

St James' church parade in High Bullen, 1958. In the foreground, left to right, are Father Thewlis, the Revd Philip Husbands, Maurice Hackett and Jim Hayward.

Steeplejacks from George Howell and Co. descend St Bartholomew's tower with the clock hands during repair work in 1948. Top to bottom: Richard Howell, George Howell senior, and George Howell junior.

An ox-roast in the Shambles, probably to celebrate the Coronation of Queen Elizabeth II on 2 June 1953. In the distance is Camp Street, looking in the direction of Camphill Lane. The function was performed by Harry Johnson, 'World Champion Ox-Roaster', from Cradley Heath.

Town hall staff Judith Farmer and Ann Hollingsworth welcome young revellers to the NALGO children's Christmas party at the town hall, 1963.

Opening day at the RSPCA clinic, Russell Street, 18 March 1969. The premises had formerly been the temporary building for H.L. Roberts' Newsagents. The horse rider is unknown but the line up left to right is Margaret Burkitt, Inspector Parker, Paul Burkitt, Marjorie Woosnam, Kenneth Brawn, Ivy Brawn and Freda Baker. The dog's name is Toffee.

Canine competitors parade in the dog show at Wodensborough High School, Hydes Road, 1977. Contestant no. 4 (on the right) is Julie Werrett. It appears the sawdust has had to be used!

Alderman Ethel Price presents school swimming shields, 1962. Mrs Price was Wednesbury's only Lady Mayor, taking office in 1950–1 and 1962–3. Her husband, Councillor George Price, was in office from 1938 to 1939.

Pupils from Wodensborough High School are pictured in 1974 with the minibus they bought and presented to the Wolverhampton branch of the Multiple Sclerosis Society. Funds were raised for worthy causes by an annual 25-mile sponsored walk.

CHAPTER NINE

LOST BUILDINGS

Oakeswell Hall, Walsall Street, pictured here in about 1950, was unusual for its lantern tower, a rare architectural feature. It was home to the Royalist Hopkins family during the Civil War, and a Cromwellian cannon ball was unearthed in the grounds during excavation of an air raid shelter during the Second World War. Sadly the ancient pile was demolished in 1962.

When T. Marshall and Company, grocers of Holyhead Road, was demolished in August 1963 family members undertook the removal themselves – to temporary premises at the delicensed Britannia Inn across the road. Elsie Jones watches from the shop entrance as Elizabeth Cooper, Sam Jones and a younger helper carry items of furniture from the old building.

Cousins Jim Hazell and Eric Buckley stand in the garden of 5 Leabrook Square, c. 1930. Behind can be seen the kiln and other buildings of the Leabrook Pottery. In the seventeenth century the town was famed for its salt-glazed vessels, known as Wedgbury Ware.

Wednesbury Central railway station, Great Western Street, pictured early in 1971 before demolition commenced. As the address suggests, this was part of Isambard Kingdom Brunel's Great Western Railway.

The platforms and track, again seen in 1971, are ironically the site of Wednesbury's brand new halt and operations depot of the Midland Metro Light Rail System, due to commence service on the former Great Western line in 1998.

This neat little building in High Bullen was a gents' urinal, built in 1905. The granite horse trough was presented by Miss Jane Handley also in 1905, and has now been moved to nearby Union Street. The cast-iron posts, which now stand outside the George Inn, were boundary markers from Thomas Telford's 1825 London to Holyhead Road improvements. The urinal was demolished on 24 October 1993.

The Armourite Metal Company produced copper jugs, posthorns and coaching lamps from 1960 until demolition in the 1980s at the former New Pack Horse Inn, Dudley Street, which was built in 1837.

Industrial giants Rubery Owen had their Research and Development Department at Church Street, seen here on 6 June 1966. This had to be removed to make way for the Northern Orbital by-pass in 1969.

The huge Old Park Works dominated the Wednesbury skyline until demolition in March 1994. Originally part of the Patent Shaft and Axletree Company, they were taken over by the Metropolitan-Cammell Carriage and Waggon Company, producing railway stock. Tanks were made here during both world wars.

Nos 25 to 28 High Bullen, when pictured in about 1967, were occupied by Joseph Glaze, jeweller and antiques dealer, William Webb, tobacconist, and Frederick Horton, corn merchant. Although the 'timber framing' visible was only paint, demolition in 1969 revealed genuine Tudor framework.

The Hollies was built in about 1820 by Whitmore Jones, owner of Wednesbury Mill, and stood on the crest of Hollies Drive. Many of Wednesbury's elite resided there during its 150 years. When demolished in about 1970, it was in use as offices for Wilkins and Mitchell, who produced the well-known Servis washing machines.

The Keep, standing in the grounds of The Hollies, was built by one-time resident Cornelius Whitehouse to celebrate his extended patent for the butt-welded tube, sometime after 1825. A round tower also stood at the entrance gates in Hollies Drive. The Georgian Gardens housing development now occupies the site.

Dolobran House, Wood Green Road, was home to the Lloyd family, distinguished industrialists, and named after their ancestral home Dolobran Hall, in the parish of Meifod near Welshpool. Pictured in 1950, it was converted to the County Commercial College in 1926. Now demolished, new housing has taken its place.

Myvod House was another Lloyd residence, which stood opposite to Dolobran. The corrupted spelling refers to their native Meifod, which means summerhouse. When photographed in 1931, it was in use as a sick babies' hostel. Nurses can be seen guarding cots placed on the terrace for fresh air. The house was demolished in the 1960s to make way for annexed college buildings.

St Bartholomew's Church School, built in 1829, is pictured awaiting demolition on 6 June 1966. Lower down Church Street can be seen the Woden Inn.

The County Metallurgical and Engineering Institute, built in 1914 and later renamed the County Technical College, stood in Walsall Street, with the main entrance in Kendrick Street. It was demolished in 1998 and a housing development now fills the site.

The Horse and Jockey public house, rebuilt in 1913, and fire station of 1899 are viewed from across the High Bullen roundabout, November 1964. Both were demolished in 1968 for the Northern Orbital by-pass.

Waterworks Cottages, Brunswick Park Road, were – as their name suggests – built to accommodate staff from the adjacent water pumping station. They are pictured here in June 1964 and have since had their roofs and upper rooms demolished, and have been converted into a lock-up unit.

The George Inn was removed from its corner position between Union Street and Upper High Street for a road widening scheme. In this photograph of 1959 its successor can just be seen to the right. Older residents still refer to The George as 'Top Wrexham', the name of a former brewery perhaps.

The Dartmouth Arms Inn, pictured here in about 1960, stood at the busy Holyhead Road and Dudley Street crossroads – a notorious accident blackspot. It was demolished in March 1963 for the construction of the aptly named Dartmouth Arms traffic island. This was also known as 'Bottom Wrexham', being in almost exact alignment with the George Inn.

The Mazeppa in Elwell Street, Mesty Croft, was named after a Polish nobleman. Licensee William Powell is seen in the doorway, c. 1930. To the left, the River Tame footbridge can just be seen. After a spell as an office, the building was demolished in 1997.

Although replaced by a modern successor in 1985, the Village Inn, Alma Street, was the last of Mesty Croft's six original public houses to retain its licence. Others included the Rising Sun, Foresters, Vine and Museum.

The Palace Cinema was showing the film *Always Goodbye*, starring Barbara Stanwyck, when this photograph of Upper High Street was taken in about 1937. The Palace was demolished in 1964.

The Rialto Cinema, Earps Lane, was originally built in 1859 as the old Theatre Royal. It had already been converted to the Midland Cinema Bingo Club when photographed on 2 February 1965. This was yet another establishment swept away for the 1969 Northern Orbital by-pass.

CHAPTER TEN

CUP FINAL

Wednesbury vocal quartet. Left to right: Bernard Silk, C.H. Keeling, J. Samways and W. Ingram-Benning, with the Leamington Spa County Vocals Challenge Cup, c. 1925.

Members of Holyhead Road Baptist FC with the Alfred Bird Challenge Cup, 1906. James Henry Allen is standing on the extreme right. Behind can be seen the Sunday school of 1881. The premises serve as a tyre-fitting bay today.

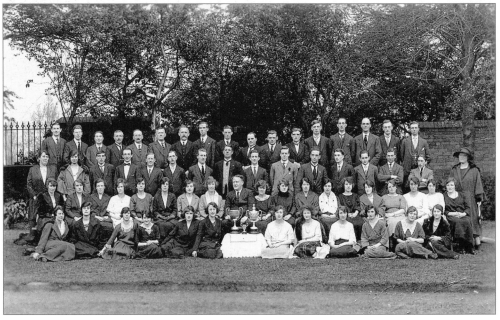

Wednesbury Choral Society proudly display three cups won in 1922. Choirmaster Ernest Amphlett sits in the centre of the second row.

Children of the Meeting Street Black and White Jazz Band had a very successful 1932 judging by the array of certificates and three cups visible.

Silver cups await presentation at the Conservative Club Annual Dinner, 1936. The Walsall Street premises were opened by Lord Windsor in 1904.

Fire service staff display trophies gained through fire and rescue competitions, at the Ladbury's Lane station, *c.* 1949. The two engines leave just enough room to squeeze into the tiny garage.

Wednesbury Civil Defence Sub-Rescue Team are presented with leather writing cases and the J.A. Stokes Rescue Trophy, won in consecutive years 1961–3. The training ground was at Murdock Road, Bilston.

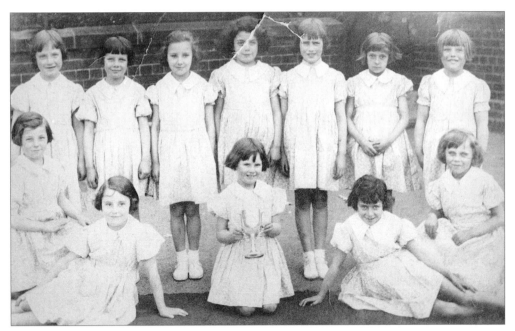

Girls from Holyhead Road Infants School proudly exhibit their country dancing cup, won in 1937 at Wolverhampton. Back row, left to right: Vera Moseley, Doreen Ford, Joan Price, Betty Wilson, Irene Smith, Margaret Shilton, Josie Goodman. Front row: Ivy Robinson, Pat Jones, Betty Owen, Vera Middlebrook and Eileen Evans.

Wednesbury Girls High School netball team at Heronville School with the senior schools cup, 1960. Presumably Heronville were their opponents.

Teacher Beryl Share presents the same netball trophy to yet another winning team member in 1962. The poodle was probably team mascot.

Wednesbury Elevens' youth team in 1955 with the season's trophy. The photograph was probably taken in the grounds of St Bartholomew's School.

Wednesbury Bridge Social Club members are pictured at the Bridge Street club, with the West Bromwich District Snooker League Cup, 1953. Back row, left to right: G. Botfield, F. Hill, T. Wood. Front row: L. Cartwright, D. Cosgrove, W. Williams.

Presentation of the Wednesbury District Crib League Cup, *c.* 1955. The picture was probably taken at Park Lane Working Men's Club.

Britannia Inn crib players pose with the Wednesbury District Cup, *c.* 1950. Frederick Noakes, top right, was licensee of the Holyhead Road pub from 1946 until 1953.

Managing Director of Prodorite Ltd, Harold Fender, pictured far right, presents William Bradley with the works fishing trophy, watched by Douglas Burrows, on 20 May 1957. Seated in the background are Arthur Gibbs and Anthony Fender. Note the bow-fronted case containing a stuffed fish.

Wednesbury Sports Union annual dinner presentation at the Anchor Hotel, Holyhead Road, 1965.
Leonard Middleton awards Ann Hollingsworth with the lawn tennis trophy, watched by, left to right,
Mary Cooper, Ann Myatt and John Ross.

Members of Wednesbury Sons of Rest, Foley Street, with the 1979 season's winnings of darts and snooker
trophies. The pictures seen on page 76 of this book hang in the background.

ACKNOWLEDGEMENTS

The author would like to express his sincere thanks to all the individuals listed below, without whose help this book would not have been possible.

Mary Beadle, Cyril Beardmore, Inga Beardmore, Revd David Kirk Beedon, Brian Beesley, Vera Best, Ann Betteridge, Frank Betteridge, Christopher Bott, Jim Boulton, Enid Bourne, John Bradley, Ray Brookes, Brian Broome, Margaret Burkitt, Paul Burkitt, Lilian Butlin, Kathleen Clarke, Margaret Cooper, Gladys Cox, Katharine Dudley, Kathleen Dunkley, Mrs M. Gibbs, Betty Golder, Brenda Greenhough, Stan Griffiths, Clara Harrison, Tony Highfield, Burt Hobbs, Mark Hooper, Michael Horton, Richard Howell, Dorothy Inett, Mrs Ingram, Sylvia King, Jean Knott, Kathleen Lewis, Marian Maczka, Tony Mallam, Janice Meacham, Bernard Minton, Margaret Nicholls, Mr and Mrs Horace Page, Dora Palmer, Olive Parker, the late Norman Pearson, the late Alison Phillips, Nellie Phillips, Stan Powell, Doreen Pugh, Molly Pym, Freda Riley, Ivy Rowley, Lilian Russell, Doreen Scott, Clarice Shore, Jill Simcox, Patricia Smith, Paul Smith, Les Stevenson, Mary Stevenson, Patricia Stevenson, Sam Stevenson, Peter Tapper-Gray, Alan Thorpe, Gladys Tromans, Hazel Turner, Betty Wardle, Dennis Warner, Mary Warner, Irene Whittaker, Rachel Wilkins, Ned Williams, Ray Wood, Lynn Yates.

The author would also like to acknowledge the courtesy of the following organisations:

Birmingham Post and Mail Limited, *Express and Star Newspapers* Limited, Sandwell Metropolitan Borough Council, St Bartholomew's Church Council, Thames Television, *Walsall Observer* Limited, Wednesbury Sons of Rest, West Midlands Fire Brigade.